P9-DVT-181

CALGARY PUBLIC LIBRARY

SEP   2015

Pebble® Plus

Royalty

Knights

by Sally Lee

Consulting Editor: Gail Saunders-Smith, PhD

Consultant: Glenn A. Steinberg, PhD
Associate Professor of English
The College of New Jersey
Ewing, New Jersey

CAPSTONE PRESS
a capstone imprint

Pebble Plus is published by Capstone Press,
1710 Roe Crest Drive, North Mankato, Minnesota 56003
www.capstonepub.com

Copyright © 2013 by Capstone Press, a Capstone imprint. All rights reserved. No part of this publication may be reproduced in whole or in part, or stored in a retrieval system, or transmitted in any form or by any means, electronic, mechanical, photocopying, recording, or otherwise, without written permission of the publisher.

Library of Congress Cataloging-in-Publication Data
Lee, Sally.
 Knights / by Sally Lee.
     p. cm.—(Pebble plus. Royalty)
 Includes bibliographical references and index.
  ISBN 978-1-62065-122-3 (library binding)
  ISBN 978-1-4765-1086-6 (eBook PDF)
1. Knights and knighthood—Juvenile literature. 2. Civilization, Medieval—Juvenile literature. I. Title.
 CR4513.L44 2013
 929.7′1—dc23
                                                                 2012030333

Editorial Credits
Erika L. Shores, editor; Juliette Peters, designer; Wanda Winch, media researcher; Jennifer Walker, production specialist

Photo Credits
AP Images: Press Association, 21; The Bridgeman Art Library: © Look and Learn/Private Collection/ Peter Jackson, 7, 9, 13, Private Collection/Gino D'Achille, 5; Corbis: Heritage Images, 17, Stapleton Collection, 11, The Print Collector, 19; Shutterstock: Anna Subbotina, red satin design, Ecelop, gold swoosh design, hardtmuth, gold frame, Kajano, cover, Nejron Photo, 1, 15, stanalex, cover castle

Note to Parents and Teachers

The Royalty set supports national social studies standards related to people, places, and culture. This book describes and illustrates knights. The images support early readers in understanding the text. The repetition of words and phrases helps early readers learn new words. This book also introduces early readers to subject-specific vocabulary words, which are defined in the Glossary section. Early readers may need assistance to read some words and to use the Table of Contents, Glossary, Read More, Internet Sites, and Index sections of the book.

Printed in China.
092012   006934LEOS13

Table of Contents

What Is a Knight?

Knights in the Middle Ages had a dangerous job. These skilled soldiers fought to protect their lord's land and castle.

A knight's training began around age 7. Boys from important families served as pages for a lord at a nearby castle.

Pages became squires

around age 14.

A squire served a knight

who taught him about fighting

and other skills.

The Life of a Knight

Knights fought their enemies
with swords and lances.
They wore armor
from head to toe. It was
hot and uncomfortable.

Knights in heavy armor needed

strong horses to carry them.

The horses also had to be quick.

Wearing armor made all knights
look alike. Each knight had
a coat of arms painted
on his shield to tell them apart.

Knights showed off their skills

by holding tournaments.

Two teams of knights

fought a pretend war.

Their battles were bloody.

17

Knights Today

A knight's skills weren't needed

after guns became common.

Armor was useless against bullets.

Regular soldiers were easier

to train.

Today a few countries still have knights. But these knights don't fight battles. Knighthood is a title given to people who serve the country in an important way.

England's Queen Elizabeth II knights Sir Simon Bryant of the Royal Air Force.

Glossary

armor—a suit made of metal or other strong material, worn to protect the body during battle

coat of arms—a set of colored symbols and designs that stand for a certain family, church, or country

lance—a long pole with a pointed metal head used as a weapon in battles

lord—a person who ruled over land given to him by a king or another important, wealthy person

Middle Ages—the period in history from the year 500 to the year 1500

page—a young boy who worked as a servant for a lord, knight, or king

squire—a young man from an important family who served as a knight's helper

sword—a weapon that has a long pointed blade fixed on a handle

tournament—a contest in which knights fought to win honor and riches

Read More

Bergin, Mark. *Knights and Castles.* It's Fun to Draw. New York: Windmill Books, 2012.

Lee, Sally. *Kings and Queens.* Royalty. North Mankato, Minn.: Capstone Press, 2013.

Stiefel, Chana. *Sweaty Suits of Armor: Could You Survive Being a Knight?* Ye Yucky Middle Ages. Berkeley Heights, N.J.: Enslow, 2012.

Internet Sites

FactHound offers a safe, fun way to find Internet sites related to this book. All of the sites on FactHound have been researched by our staff.

Here's all you do:

Visit *www.facthound.com*

Type in this code: 9781620651223

Super-cool stuff!

Check out projects, games and lots more at
www.capstonekids.com

Index

Word Count: 187
Grade: 1
Early-Intervention Level: 19